But Where Do You Get Your Protein?!

Healthy Eating The VEGAN Way

by

Sasha Carr

Illustrated by Joel Ray Pellerin

To order additional copies of this book, contact:
Xlibris LLC
1-800-455-039
www.xlibris.com.au
Orders@Xlibris.com.au

Abstaining from meat, dairy, eggs and honey, vegans are extreme (they're a little... funny). I mean really, there isn't even any *fish* in their tea time dish! But I ask that you pause to question this assumption as, actually, your body digests plants with gumption.

But you need protein, people will protest. *Protein comes from meat* they'll say (intentions at their best). You'll be pleased to hear that what we fear is groundless after all; fruit and veg, seeds, nuts and *beans* can make us strong and tall. Fresh juices, smoothies, soups, desserts are some of what you'll eat. Get creative, keep it fresh; give yourself a treat. Your brain will thrive, your body too, protein won't be lacking; and with so many scrumptious foods your lips will soon be smacking.

Compassion you will start to feel as you fuel your body every meal. You *do* need calcium for strong bones and teeth, but from *dairy*?! That's for *calves* (not you) so be wary. Calcium from leafy greens won't be boring by any means; spinach, rhubarb, lettuce, kale (with corn, nuts and seeds—you're not a snail!). Leafy greens, almonds, figs and *mango* ensure ample calcium so strong bones can grow.

Don't be scared to break the mould, you know your mind; be strong, be bold. Animals are not alive simply so that *you* can thrive. You *don't* need fish, lamb, chicken or cow; what great news, go vegan now! You're really *not* a carnivore, responding to this claim's a chore: your teeth aren't sharp, you have no claws, you lack the speed and trap-like jaws.

Eggs are a favourite I think you'd agree; scrambled or boiled, for brekkie or tea. But every egg you choose to buy supports a practice that would make you cry. Free range, organic, caged (or not) the rule applies to the lot. Male chicks are of no use you see (they lay no eggs for the industry): at one day old the boys are sorted, their lives from that point are quickly thwarted. *You* have the power to support or oppose those practices that make you crinkle your nose. You know what feels right and what hurts your heart, so put healthy, delicious, whole foods in your cart.

Factory farming blows my mind, how can humans *be* so unkind towards feeling, breathing, sentient creatures that *don't* differ hugely from us in their features. Two lungs to breathe, two eyes to see, a nose to smell, legs run free. Animals use their brain to think and (again like us) when they fart? They stink! Perhaps they soar high, use their wings to fly or use fins, gills and scales to dive with the whales. However they move, wherever they live, a chance to live free, to them we must give. All animal hearts beat the same, this is their *life*—it isn't a game. They feel fear and they feel pain, their freedom they deserve to gain.

Goji berries, chia seeds, mushrooms, fruit and kale will satisfy your body's needs, ensure your skin's not pale. Mix these in a smoothie (throw them in the blender); skin clear, eyes bright, your body svelte and slender. It's healthy, filling, wholesome and sweet; add frozen berries for a nice cold treat.

Health *is* attainable by one and by all but first we need an overhaul. Scientists have found meat, eggs, milk and *cheese* to be linked to every major disease. Obesity, diabetes, cancer, a sick heart; it all depends on our nutrition chart. Animal protein has too much fat, it's too acidic and not only that it has added cholesterol yet we make our own; so avoid eating animals and eat that which is grown.

Iron is crucial for healthy blood, as it runs through your veins with a silent *thud thud*; so eat spinach, pumpkin, tomato and beans; quinoa seeds and collard greens; brown rice, oatmeal, mangoes, cherries; dried fruit, nuts, melon, berries. On the run and need a snack? Put bananas or carrots into your pack.

Juicing veggies is easy you know; nutrients absorbed fast not slow. Carrot and apple and ginger is yummy, a protein hit that fills your tummy. "Green juices" are popular for improving your health; the eating revolution arriving by stealth!

Kale is a super food to have in your life; a boost for your body if your health is in strife. With calcium, iron and vitamin C, plenty of goodness convinced even me. With fibre and protein, antioxidants too, this green leafy vegetable will help you right through. Eat it in a salad, in a soup or on some pasta; or make yourself a smoothie to ingest it even faster.

Lentils and beans with wholegrain rice are good for digestion (absolutely, no question). They're good for your heart, your bowel and your mood, they're warm and they're filling, a real comfort food. Fibre, iron, calcium, protein, all are contained in one little bean.

Mammals make milk when they have a *baby*. A cow is no different to us so just maybe when *we* move on to solid food we should drink *plant*-based milk and not *be* so rude as to take the milk that's meant for the calf: it's *not* a necessity, not even by half. Cows too are mums but their young they must *lose* just so veal and dairy *we* can choose. In this country, every year, countless calves will perish (the industry won't let them drink the milk that *we* so cherish). Plant-based milks are the kind way to go; cruelty free they nourish you to grow.

Nutrients (you'll find) are the key, to a strong and healthy you and me. But are you being your wisest self when you choose your products from the shelf? If we gave the grains we feed to our food to our fellow human beings then think of it, dude: no more starvation, diminished disease, compassion and sharing, kindness and caring. No longer would animals be mass produced, their suffering at our hands greatly reduced.

Omega-3 for every cell helps your body function well. Forget the eggs, the meat, the fish, completely change your standard dish. Because unlike plants fish *do* feel pain (of course they do, they too have a brain) and chia seeds, walnuts, beans and flaxseed also meet that oily need.

Protein *is* important (for your muscles, your blood, the lot); but the correct information we simply haven't got. How much protein do we actually need? 10% of calories, so let's check our greed. Too much animal protein and our systems run amok; we get rather sick which really is bad luck. Fruits and veg, nuts and grain, legumes and seeds do protein contain.

Quinoa (*Keen-wah*), wow, what an amazing seed: nutty, versatile; a super food indeed. Quinoa porridge to start your day is protein-rich to fuel your play. Adding walnuts, dried fruit and *flaxseed* provides a yummy breakfast indeed. Quinoa comes in black, it comes in red, it comes in white; for a stir fry or a salad with quinoa muffins to delight.

Rainbow colours every day ensure a balanced diet; treat your taste buds, try new things, keep tummy rumblings quiet. Eat sweet potato, carrots, eggplant, avocado; mango, bananas, strawberries and tomato; raspberries and blueberries, pineapple and pear; kiwi fruit and coconuts, some lychees thrown in there. Capsicum in orange, in red or in green; such a range of colours on your plate there's never been.

Strong immune systems are an unexpected plus; eat those plant-based whole foods and with illness you won't fuss. But remember to eat in colours (a rainbow!) as bland vegan junk food won't cut it you know. If you were to exist on biscuits, chips and cake it wouldn't just be boring but a costly mistake. You'd have no energy, your body wouldn't thrive; you'd be living alright but not feeling alive. Your sickness or your health you *can* largely control, but it depends (absolutely) on what goes in your bowl.

There's more to being vegan than what goes in your belly; so watch the products closely when they're advertised on telly. Leather's really cow skin and wool is meant for sheep, feathers in your eiderdown warm you as you sleep. Your shoes, your belts, your winter wear reflect how much you truly care; so pay attention, use your eyes and seek out those words that would disguise.

Understanding our bodies, understanding what they need, can dispel any myths and help us to succeed. Yes, it's important to choose well when we eat. No, our healthiest option is *not* dairy, eggs or meat. For minerals and vitamins which best is the source? The answer, you'll find, is plants (of course).

Vitamin B12 for your blood and your brain; but meat's not what's needed—let me explain. Unwashed organic fruit and veg with some soil left on the edge, nutritional yeast on oats and seeds or fortified plant milk meet B12 needs.

Whole foods, sunshine, water (*that's* what our bodies need); so let's eat plant-based options and let the animals be freed. Our fellow earthlings *do* require that we respect their most basic desire (to be happy and free from suffering). Watch your dog wag her tail, or defend you bravely when you get mail; dogs really are no different at all from *any* animal to fly, swim or crawl. We'll eat a pig but not a cat. Seriously? What's up with that?!

eXcuses you really have no more, you are *not* a true carnivore. A carnivore won't cook and season; she'll devour her meat, fresh and raw! You *can* be strong without meat, dairy, cheese (and don't forget the eggs, if you please). Too much animal protein *can* make you sick, so jump on board with wholefoods, quick!

Yummy treats to celebrate a birthday girl or boy; vegan kids aren't left behind, there's ample to enjoy. To bake some scrumptious biscuits or a massive chocolate cake there are three simple tweaks (some changes) you will want to make: use plant-based milk (not cow's), plant-based spread (not butter); and one more trick before (you'll find) delighted sounds you'll utter: animal products are not a treat so replace the *eggs* before adding heat (with banana, apple sauce or soaked chia seeds—no remorse, no regrets, just what a vegan needs).

Zoos and circuses? Don't get me started; the cruelty there can be brutal, cold hearted. Eat well, play often, celebrate life; but stop animal suffering (so widespread, so rife). We don't need to eat them, we don't need their eggs, we *don't* need the milk of those on four legs. Put down your knife, pick up your fork; your belly full of plants (not pork). Eat plant-based whole foods (they're cruelty free): take off your blinkers it's time to see.

CPSIA information can be obtained
at www.ICGtesting.com
Printed in the USA
LVIC04n1427310814
401737LV00014B/64

9 781499 010046